Muffins

a cookbook

by Joan and Marilyn

OUR THANKS...

— to our families who tasted, then cheerfully commented on endless dozens of muffins.

— to friends and relatives who encouraged and cajoled us.

— to Susan Bidinosti who designed the cover and did the illustrations and layout.

— to Perry D'Elia and the staff of Pear Creative. Their enthusiasm and patience contributed immeasurably to the completion of the book.

Publishers: Muffins Publishing Inc.

Joan Bidinosti (519) 433-0807
2 Westview Drive,
London, Ontario N6A 2Y3

Marilyn Wearring (519) 660-0545
R.R. #5,
London, Ontario N6A 4B9

Canadian Cataloguing in Publication Data
Bidinosti, Joan
 Muffins: a cookbook
ISBN 0-9691345-0-9
1. Muffins.   I. Wearring, Marilyn   II. Title.
TX769.B44   641.8'15   C83-00457-2

Printed by PEAR CREATIVE LTD.
39 Charterhouse Crescent, London, Ontario N5W 5V3 • (519) 659-3528

Printed in Canada

Introduction

The challenge to create a muffin cookbook was irresistible. We are not professionals - we have no credentials as food columnists. Rather we are wives/mothers - each with four teen-age (more-or-less) children who have eaten hundreds of our muffins. This book is our reply to, "Mum, you should write a muffin cookbook".

Our book includes many popular favorites. Recipes were given to us by friends and relatives; others were gleaned from cookbooks, magazines and newspapers (often modified) and many were developed by us. We have tested them all.

As we collected and tested, we became increasingly aware that muffins have taken on a new image. Young and old are eating them for breakfast, packing them in lunches and munching them for snacks. Furthermore, the trend towards a more active lifestyle and improved eating habits has heightened the interest in nutritional content. As a result, many of our selections emphasize nutrition, others are primarily confections.

Hopefully the novice cook will be enticed and encouraged, while the experienced baker will be tempted to experiment. We have tried to present the recipes clearly and simply so that you, the reader, will *use* and enjoy "MUFFINS... a cookbook".

Joan Bidinosti
Marilyn Wearring

Muffins ... A to Z

Basic Muffin

TEMP. 400° F
TIME 20 minutes
MAKES 10 - 12 large muffins

A basic recipe included to illustrate the standard muffin method. Vary it as you wish by adding fruit, nuts, chocolate chips, etc.

1½ **cups all-purpose flour**
½ **cup white sugar**
2 **tsp baking powder**
½ **tsp salt**
1 **egg**
½ **cup milk**
¼ **cup vegetable oil**

1. Heat oven to 400° F. Rack in middle of oven.
2. Dark pans may require slightly lower temperature or shorter baking time than shiny pans.
3. Grease muffin cups or use paper baking cups.
4. Sift dry ingredients together in bowl.
5. In separate bowl beat egg slightly with fork. Stir in milk and oil.
6. Make a well in dry mixture and pour in liquid.
7. Stir until moistened only. Batter should be lumpy - do not overmix.
8. Fill muffin cups two-thirds full and bake 20 minutes.

 Always read entire recipe before you begin.

Applesauce Oatmeal Prune

TEMP. 400° F
TIME 20 minutes
MAKES 11 large muffins

*Eat your breakfast as you run out the door...
a handful of flavor!*

¾ **cup all-purpose flour**
½ **tsp cinnamon**
½ **tsp salt**
¼ **tsp nutmeg**
1 **Tbsp baking powder**
1¼ **cups rolled oats**
¾ **cup chopped prunes**
½ **cup brown sugar**
½ **cup vegetable oil**
1 **egg**
1 **cup applesauce**

1. Sift first five ingredients into bowl.
2. Stir in oats, prunes and brown sugar.
3. Beat oil and egg together. Add applesauce.
4. Pour into dry mixture. Stir to blend.
5. Fill muffin cups and bake.

Whole Wheat Applesauce

TEMP. 350°F
TIME 20 - 25 minutes
MAKES 12 large muffins

Developed using stoneground flour. Better if you "grind your own" as Bill does.

- ⅓ **cup vegetable oil**
- ⅓ **cup milk**
- 1 **tsp vanilla**
- 1 **or 2 eggs**
- ⅔ **cup applesauce (rhubarb sauce)**
- ½ **cup brown sugar**
- 2 **cups whole-wheat flour**
- 2 **tsp baking powder**
- ¼ **tsp salt**

1. In small bowl mix all wet ingredients.
2. In large bowl combine all dry ingredients.
3. Add wet to dry. Stir just until blended.
4. Fill muffin cups and bake.

 Instead of applesauce try ½ cup raisins, dates or berries and increase milk by about ½ cup.

Add spice with a dash of cinnamon and nutmeg.

Apple Surprise

TEMP. 375° F
TIME 20 - 25 minutes
MAKES 18 medium muffins

Read recipe before starting...
wonderfully different... well worth the extra effort
and expense.

1 **can pie-sliced apples (19 oz.)**	1½ **cups all-purpose flour**
½ **cup white sugar (first amount)**	1 **tsp baking soda**
1 **Tbsp cinnamon (first amount)**	1 **tsp baking powder**
¼ **cup chopped walnuts**	½ **tsp salt**
½ **cup butter**	½ **tsp cinnamon (second amount)**
½ **cup white sugar (second amount)**	¼ **tsp cardamom (optional)**
2 **eggs**	¼ **tsp almond extract**
	1 **cup grated cheddar cheese**
	¼ **cup strong coffee**

1. Drain apples. Reserve 18 slices. Chop remainder.
2. Sprinkle some sugar and cinnamon (first amounts) on 18 slices. Mix rest with walnuts.
3. Cream butter, sugar (second amount) & eggs.
4. Sift in dry ingredients. Mix to blend.
5. Stir in chopped apple, cheese & coffee.
6. Fill muffin cups ¼ full.
7. *Press 1 sugared apple slice into each cup.*
8. *Fill muffin cups with remainder of batter.*
9. *Sprinkle with sugar, cinnamon, nut mixture and bake.*

3

Chunky Apple

TEMP. 375° F
TIME 20 minutes
MAKES 10 large muffins

'Chunks' of apple... rather than grated... make these extra special.

¼ **cup vegetable oil**
¾ **cup brown sugar**
1 **egg**
1 **Tbsp cream**
1½ **cups chopped apple (peeled)**
½ **cup raisins**
1 **cup all-purpose flour (or whole-wheat)**
¾ **tsp baking soda**
¾ **tsp salt**
1 **tsp baking powder**
¼ **tsp cinnamon**
¼ **tsp nutmeg**
TOPPING MIXTURE
1 **tsp cinnamon**
1½ **Tbsp white sugar**

1. In large bowl beat oil, sugar, egg and cream.
2. Stir in apple and raisins.
3. Sift in dry ingredients. Stir to blend.
4. Fill muffin cups.
5. Sprinkle topping mixture on batter and bake.

Blender Apple

TEMP. 375° F
TIME 30 minutes
MAKES 11 large muffins

One of the easiest muffins you'll make... blended red skin adds vitamins, flavor and color.

1½ **cups all-purpose flour**
½ **cup whole-wheat flour**
2 **tsp baking powder**
¼ **tsp baking soda**
½ **tsp salt**
¼ **tsp cinnamon**
⅔ **cup milk**
1 **egg**
⅓ **cup vegetable oil**
¾ **cup brown sugar**
2 **medium red apples (cored, unpeeled)**
¼ **cup nuts**

1. Sift flour, baking powder, soda, salt and cinnamon into large bowl.
2. Into electric blender put milk, egg, oil, sugar, nuts and apple (cut in eighths). Blend well.
3. Pour into flour mixture. Stir only until mixed.
4. Fill muffin cups and bake.

 Before baking sprinkle batter in muffin cups with sugar and cinnamon.

5

Easy Banana

TEMP. 350° F
TIME 20 - 25 minutes
MAKES 12 large muffins

If time is limited this is a speedy and delicious treat from the ABSOLON farm.

1 **cup mashed bananas (2 or 3 medium)**
1 **cup miracle whip dressing**
¾ **cup white sugar**
2 **cups flour (⅔ C whole-wheat, 1⅓ C all-purpose)**
2 **tsp baking soda**
½ **tsp salt**

1. In medium large bowl beat bananas.
2. Beat in sugar and salad dressing.
3. Stir in flour, soda and salt just until moistened.
4. Fill muffin cups and bake.

Joan's Banana

TEMP. 400°F
TIME 20 - 25 minutes
MAKES 14 large muffins

An old favorite from Flin Flon... Joan's family has eaten hundreds of these.

1 **cup white sugar**
½ **cup vegetable oil**
2 **eggs**
3 **bananas**
3 **Tbsp sour cream or (soured milk)**
1 **tsp baking soda**
2 **cups all-purpose flour**

1. With electric mixer, beat sugar and oil.
2. Add eggs, then bananas. Beat thoroughly.
3. Dissolve soda in sour cream.
4. Turn mixer to low speed. Slowly add soda-cream to banana mixture.
5. Sift in flour and continue to mix gently until blended.
6. Fill muffin cups and bake.

 If bananas are small we use four.

Banana 'n Peanut

TEMP. 400°F
TIME 15 minutes
MAKES 12 large muffins

A nutritious recipe from "Action Nanaimo" for peanut and banana lovers..

1½ **cups whole-wheat flour**
2 **tsp baking powder**
½ **tsp baking soda**
¼ **tsp cinnamon**
¼ **tsp nutmeg**
½ **cup brown sugar**
3 **large, ripe bananas**
1 **egg**
⅓ **cup vegetable oil**
2 **Tbsp crunchy peanut butter**
½ **cup coarsely chopped peanuts**

1. In large bowl, stir dry ingredients with a fork.
2. In small bowl, mash bananas. (Or purée in blender)
3. Whisk (or blend) oil, peanut butter and egg with banana.
4. Stir banana mixture into dry ingredients with nuts.
5. Fill muffin cups and bake.

TEMP. 450° F
TIME 12 - 15 minutes
MAKES 10 - 12 large muffins

Let your young cook try this recipe... so quick and easy... just one of each ingredient.

1 **Tbsp shortening**
1 **cup brown sugar**
1 **egg**
1 **cup natural bran**
1 **cup all-purpose flour**
1 **tsp baking soda**
  pinch of salt
1 **cup raisins (washed)**
1 **cup sour milk or buttermilk**

1. Cream shortening, sugar and egg in large bowl.
2. Combine dry ingredients.
3. Sift in dry ingredients alternately with sour milk.
4. Add raisins and stir until moistened.
5. Fill muffin cups and bake.

Moist Bran

TEMP. 375°F
TIME 20 - 25 minutes
MAKES 3 dozen large muffins
(Refrigerator Batch)

Ultra convenient to have batter in the fridge...hot muffins in twenty minutes.

1	**cup shortening (or margarine)**
2	**cups white sugar (or ½ C molasses, 1¼ C sugar)**
2	**cups natural bran**
4	**eggs**
3	**cups buttermilk**
1	**Tbsp baking powder**
3¾	**cups all-purpose flour**
1	**Tbsp baking soda**
½	**cup hot water**

1. In very large bowl, cream shortening and sugar.
2. Stir in bran, eggs, buttermilk, flour and baking powder.
3. Dissolve soda in ½ C hot water and pour on top of first mixture.
4. After 1 minute mix together.
5. **Cover and keep cool in fridge for 24 hours before baking.**
6. Batter will keep up to 2 weeks in fridge.

 Add 1 cup or more of cut-up dates or raisins or currants or prunes.

TEMP. 425° F
TIME 15 minutes
MAKES 4 dozen large muffins
(Refrigerator Batch)

Weightlifter Roscoe's favorite because of its rich "healthy" flavor... "power" in every bite.

6 **cups all-bran cereal**
2 **cups boiling water**
1 **cup vegetable oil**
1 **cup molasses**
4 **eggs**
4 **cups buttermilk (1 litre)**
2 **cups uncooked, cut-up prunes, dates or raisins**
5 **cups sifted all-purpose flour**
2 **Tbsp baking soda**
1 **tsp salt**

1. In **extra large** bowl, mix cereal with boiling water. Allow to cool.
2. In small bowl (or 4-cup measure), beat oil, molasses and eggs with a fork.
3. Stir egg mixture into bran in bowl with buttermilk and prunes.
4. Sift in flour, soda and salt. Stir just until blended.
5. **Cover and keep cool in fridge for 24 hours before baking.**
6. Do not remix.

 For variety Joan "throws in" some sesame seeds and currants at baking time.

Yogurt Bran

TEMP. 350° F
TIME 35 minutes
MAKES 2 dozen large muffins

Yogurt adds a special flavor. Gary recommends these as #1 with blueberries.

2 **cups yogurt (plain)**
2 **tsp baking soda**
1 **cup brown sugar or less to taste**
2 **eggs**
1 **cup vegetable oil**
2 **cups natural bran**
2 **tsp vanilla**
2 **cups all-purpose flour**
4 **tsp baking powder**
½ **tsp salt**
1 **cup blueberries or raisins or nuts**

1. Measure yogurt into medium bowl. Mix in soda and set aside. (Don't leave too long.)
2. In large bowl beat together eggs, sugar, oil.
3. Stir in bran and vanilla.
4. Sift together flour, baking powder, salt and add to sugar mixture alternately with yogurt.
5. Fold in fruit or nuts.
6. Fill muffin cups and bake.

Marilyn's Blueberry

TEMP. 400°F
TIME 20 minutes
MAKES 12 large muffins

From a friend in B.C., but blueberries and muffins go together in any province.

2 **eggs**
1 **cup milk**
¼ **cup melted butter (or margarine)**
1½ **cups all-purpose flour**
3 **tsp baking powder**
½ **tsp salt**
2 **Tbsp white sugar**
1 **cup blueberries**
¼ **cup flour**
½ **cup white sugar**

1. In small bowl, beat eggs, milk, butter.
2. In large bowl, mix flour, baking powder, salt and the 2 Tbsp sugar.
3. Stir liquid ingredients into dry.
4. Gently fold in mixture of blueberries, sugar and flour.
5. Fill muffin cups and bake.

13

Cranberry Yogurt

TEMP. 400° F
TIME 20 minutes
MAKES 12 large muffins

*Friends are always asking for this recipe...
use whole cranberries if in a hurry.*

1 **cup rolled oats**
1 **cup yogurt**
½ **cup vegetable oil**
¾ **cup brown sugar**
1 **egg**
1 **cup all-purpose flour**
1 **tsp salt**
½ **tsp baking soda**
1 **tsp baking powder**
1 **cup cranberries (chop in half)**
  (or blueberries)

1. Soak oats in yogurt.
2. Add oil sugar and egg. Beat well.
3. Sift in flour, salt, soda, baking powder.
4. Before stirring, sprinkle cranberries over
   flour mixture.
5. Stir to blend.
6. Fill muffin cups and bake.

 Instead of berries try dried currants...
always available.

14

Cherry Surprise

TEMP. 425°F
TIME 15 - 20 minutes
MAKES 12 large muffins

A cherry confection... an afternoon 'sweet' for the office or tea table.

- 2 **cups all-purpose flour**
- ⅓ **cup white sugar**
- 1 **Tbsp baking powder**
- ½ **tsp baking soda**
- ½ **tsp salt**
- ¼ **cup butter (or margarine)**
- 1 **cup plain yogurt**
- ¼ **cup milk**
- 1 **egg**
- ½ **tsp vanilla**
- ⅓ **cup cherry pie filling**

1. Sift dry ingredients into large bowl.
2. Melt butter. Remove from heat.
3. Stir yogurt, milk, egg, vanilla and butter together.
4. Stir butter mixture into dry ingredients.
5. Fill **well greased** muffin pans half full.
6. Place about a tsp of cherry pie filling on batter in each cup. Top with remaining batter.
7. Bake until golden.

 Instead of pie filling... try cranberry sauce or 1" cube of cream cheese and jelly or walnut half and a cherry.

15

Maraschino Cherry

TEMP. 375° F
TIME 25 minutes (15 min./small)
MAKES 12 large muffins (24 small)

Bake the small size for afternoon tea...
add calories with almond-flavored icing!

¾ **cup milk**
3 **Tbsp maraschino cherry juice**
¼ **cup vegetable oil**
1 **egg**
2 **cups all-purpose flour**
1 **Tbsp baking powder**
1 **tsp salt**
½ **cup white sugar**
⅓ **cup maraschino cherries (chopped)**
¼ **cup chopped almonds**

1. Beat together milk, juice, oil and egg.
2. Sift in dry ingredients.
3. Before mixing, add cherries and nuts.
4. Stir to blend.
5. Fill muffin cups and bake.

Christmas Cake Leftovers

TEMP. 400° F
TIME 20 - 25 minutes
MAKES 12 large muffins

A dandy way to use your extra candied and dried fruits... use 1 cup of any combination.

1 **cup all-bran cereal**
1 **cup milk**
1 **egg**
¼ **cup vegetable oil**
⅓ **cup mixed peel**
⅓ **cup candied cherries (chopped)**
⅓ **cup chopped nuts**
1 **tsp vanilla**
1 **cup all-purpose flour**
1 **cup white sugar**
3 **tsp baking powder**
½ **tsp salt**
1½ **tsp cinnamon**
½ **tsp nutmeg**
½ **tsp ginger**
¼ **tsp cloves**
¼ **tsp mace**

1. Combine all-bran and milk. Let stand until most of the moisture is absorbed.
2. Beat in egg and oil.
3. Stir in fruit, nuts and vanilla.
4. Sift in remaining ingredients. Stir to blend.
5. Fill muffin cups and bake.

17

Chocolate Chips 'n Bran

TEMP. 375°F
TIME 20 minutes
MAKES 12 large muffins

What a combination... we'll soon have everyone eating bran!

1¾ **cups all-purpose flour**
5 **tsp baking powder**
¾ **tsp salt**
1 **cup white sugar**
⅓ **cup chocolate chips (or butterscotch)**
1¼ **cups natural bran**
2 **eggs, well beaten**
1 **cup milk**
1 **tsp vanilla**
½ **cup vegetable oil**

1. Sift together first four ingredients.
2. Stir in chips and bran.
3. Mix together last four ingredients.
4. Add to flour mixture. Stir to blend.
5. Fill muffin cups and bake.

Choco-Wheat Germ

TEMP. 350°F
TIME 25 minutes (20 min./small)
MAKES 12 large muffins (24 small)

Developed from an old cake recipe... wheat germ and carob chips add an extra dimension.

½ **cup shortening at room temp.**
  (or margarine or lard)
⅔ **cup white sugar**
1 **egg**
1 **tsp vanilla**
1½ **cups all-purpose flour**
1 **tsp baking soda**
3 **Tbsp cocoa**
½ **tsp salt**
1 **cup sour milk or buttermilk**
½ **cup wheat germ**
½ **cup carob chips (or choc. chips)**

1. In large bowl, cream shortening, sugar, egg and vanilla.
2. Sift together flour, soda, cocoa and salt.
3. Stir in dry ingredients alternately with sour milk.
4. Mix in wheat germ and chips.
5. Fill muffin cups and bake.

Carrot etc.

TEMP. 400°F
TIME 20 minutes
MAKES 12 large muffins

Crunchy... a special combination... taste terrific.

1 **cup all-purpose flour**	¼ **cup chopped almonds**
2 **tsp baking powder**	¼ **cup chopped apricots**
1 **tsp baking soda**	¾ **cup grated carrot**
½ **tsp salt**	**Grated rind of**
½ **tsp cinnamon**	**1 orange**
1 **cup natural bran**	1 **cup buttermilk**
¼ **cup wheat germ**	**(or soured milk)**
¾ **cup brown sugar**	¼ **cup vegetable oil**
2 **Tbsp sesame seeds**	1 **egg**

1. Sift together flour, baking powder, soda, salt & cinnamon.
2. Stir in bran, wheat germ, brown sugar.
3. Stir in sesame seeds, almonds, apricots, grated carrot & orange rind.
4. Beat buttermilk, oil and egg together.
5. Pour into dry ingredients and stir to moisten.
6. Fill muffin cups and bake.

Carrot Prune

TEMP. 375° F
TIME 20 minutes
MAKES 18 large muffins

Like an old-fashioned 'spring tonic'... surely good for whatever ails you!

3 **eggs**
1/3 **cup brown sugar**
1/2 **cup molasses**
2/3 **cup vegetable oil**
1 **cup chopped prunes**
1 **cup shredded carrot**
2 **cups natural bran**
1/2 **cup wheat germ**
2 **cups all-purpose flour**
2 **tsp baking powder**
1 **tsp baking soda**
1 **tsp salt**
1 1/4 **cups milk**
TOPPING
2 **Tbsp brown sugar**
2 **Tbsp chopped walnuts**

1. Beat eggs and sugar together.
2. Stir in molasses & oil.
3. Add prunes, carrot, bran & wheat germ.
4. Sift flour, baking powder, soda and salt.
5. Add alternately with milk.
6. Fill muffin cups, sprinkle batter with nut topping and bake.

21

Carrot Pineapple

TEMP. 400° F
TIME 20 minutes
MAKES 12 large muffins

*A very popular recipe... like mini carrot cakes...
for 'best' top with a cream-cheese icing.*

1½ **cups all-purpose flour**
1 **cup white sugar**
1 **tsp baking soda**
1 **tsp baking powder**
1 **tsp cinnamon**
½ **tsp salt**
2 **eggs**
1 **tsp vanilla**
⅔ **cup vegetable oil**
1 **cup grated carrots**
½ **cup crushed pineapple with juice**

1. Sift dry ingredients into bowl.
2. Beat together eggs, vanilla & oil.
3. Add to flour mixture.
4. Add carrots, pineapple and juice. Mix well.
5. Fill muffin cups and bake.

Cornflake

TEMP. 425°F
TIME 20 minutes
MAKES 12 large muffins

Good for a kindergarten snack.

1 egg
1 cup buttermilk (or soured milk)
¼ cup vegetable oil
1 cup raisins
1 Tbsp grated orange rind
½ cup brown sugar
2 cups coarsely crushed cornflakes
1 cup all-purpose flour
2 tsp baking powder
½ tsp baking soda
½ tsp salt

1. Beat egg, buttermilk & oil in large bowl.
2. Stir in raisins, orange rind & sugar.
3. Blend in cornflakes.
4. Into this mixture, sift remaining ingredients.
5. Stir to blend.
6. Fill muffin cups and bake.

23

Honey Cornmeal

TEMP. 400° F
TIME 20 minutes
MAKES 12 large muffins

Lovely and light, but don't over-bake.

⅓ **cup raisins (or more)**
1 **cup cornmeal**
1½ **cups buttermilk**
1⅓ **cups all-purpose flour**
1 **tsp baking powder**
1 **tsp baking soda**
½ **tsp salt**
1 **egg**
½ **cup vegetable oil**
½ **cup honey**

1. Pour boiling water over raisins.
2. Combine cornmeal with 1 C buttermilk.
3. Into large bowl, sift dry ingredients.
4. In medium bowl, beat egg, oil, honey and remaining buttermilk.
5. Add liquid mixture to cornmeal and buttermilk.
6. Stir liquid mixture into dry. Add drained raisins.
7. Fill muffin cups and bake.

24

MUFFINS MADE EASY...

— pre-heat oven to recommended temperature
— grease muffin pans (insides & tops) or use a non-stick cooking spray or line pans with paper baking cups (our preference — no clean-up!)
— be adventurous — try variations but be aware that substitutions may change character of muffins. (If *you* like the result, does it matter if the muffins are not light, even-textured and high?)
— usually, dry and liquid ingredients are mixed thoroughly *but separately.* When combined, the batter is stirred just enough to moisten ingredients (lumpy)... overmixing causes toughness and tunnels.
— fill muffin cups *at least* ¾ full or to the top if you want big muffins. We use *large-size* paper baking cups.
— baking times are approximate; muffin is done if it is lightly browned and springs back when gently touched.
— if paper cups are used, paper often peels more easily after cooling.

STORING...

— airtight plastic containers will keep muffins *very* moist; a bonus if your muffins are dry! Refrigeration is advised if storing for more than two or three days.
— metal containers are not as airtight so better for very moist muffins.

FREEZING...

— Muffins freeze well if cooled completely and placed in airtight plastic container or wrap. Double your recipe... freeze half.

RE-HEATING...

— when taken directly from freezer, unwrap and heat in 350⁰ F oven for 10-15 minutes.
— to refresh a muffin, wrap in foil and heat in toaster oven for 5 minutes.

SUBSTITUTIONS...

— 1 cup cake flour = 1 cup less 2 Tbsp. all-purpose flour.
— 1 cup milk   = $\frac{1}{3}$ cup instant milk powder mixed
                           with dry ingredients + 1 cup water
                           mixed with liquid ingredients

— 1 cup buttermilk = substitute $\frac{1}{3}$ cup instant buttermilk
                           powder for instant milk powder in
                           the above method

— 1 cup sour milk = 1 Tbsp vinegar plus
                           sweet milk to make 1 cup.

SUGAR CONTENT...

You may find some recipes too sweet or not sweet enough for your taste. Experiment with sweetness by adding or subtracting $\frac{1}{4}$ to $\frac{1}{2}$ cup sugar. Be aware sugar content alters texture.

FRESH & HOT MUFFINS FOR GUESTS...

— have dry and liquid ingredients mixed in separate bowls. As guests arrive, quickly combine and pop into oven.

EXTRA NUTRITION...
(Cornell Triple-Rich Formula)

Before you measure each cup of flour required in your recipe, place in the bottom of the cup-measure:

    1 Tbsp soya flour
    1 Tbsp dry milk powder
    1 tsp wheat germ

Fill the cup with all-purpose flour and repeat for each cup o flour required. This mix will increase protein, calcium and vitamin E content and will make little difference to the performance of the flour or the finished flavor.

BAKING TIPS

— to fill muffin cups use a spring-type ice cream scoop or a ¼ cup that has been used to measure oil.

— too much batter for a pan of 12? — use a ¼ or ⅓ stainless steel measuring cup or a pyrex custard cup or an aluminum-foil tart form — or buy a muffin pan for 6!

— freeze over-ripe **bananas** — buy them on the "reduced" table and throw them in the freezer —let them thaw on the counter for 1½ hours. They look terrible but once peeled they're fine for baking.

— keep **nuts** in the freezer — a great way to keep them fresh and no thawing necessary.

— freeze grated **rind** from oranges and lemons in small plastic yogurt cups.

— chop **raisins** occasionally — different flavor and texture. (Especially good when raisins and nuts are chopped together.)

— **oats** used in our recipes are the 'quick-cooking' type.

— **prunes** used are the pitted variety — no more expensive when you consider the weight of the pits — and ultra convenient.

— **milk powders** are economical and convenient if refrigerator space is limited.

— substitute **dates** for raisins in any of the recipes. Often **dates** are less expensive.

— if **whole wheat flour** is sifted — bran from flour will be left in sifter. Be sure to tip it into flour mixture.

— for best flavor store **whole wheat flour, wheat germ** and **natural bran** in refrigerator. (Flour stores well in freezer.)

WHY NOT TRY...

a small tart pan to bake tiny muffins (about 5 minutes less baking time) — great for pre-schoolers — or to bake a variety for a coffee party.

TOPPINGS... for added flavor and interest

Before baking... turn batter into muffin cups and top with one of the following.

— sugar mixed with a little orange or lemon peel
— sugar mixed with cinnamon and/or nuts
— sesame or poppy seeds

After baking... while muffins are still hot, try one of these.

— sprinkle with icing sugar
— 2 Tbsp lemon juice and 4 Tbsp sugar spooned over muffins and returned to oven for 3 minutes
— dip top of muffin in melted butter, then sugar (with spice)
— paint top with jelly or marmalade

Broiler Icing:
3 Tbsp melted butter   1/4 cup chopped nuts
1/4 cup brown sugar   2 Tbsp cream
1/4 cup coconut   1/4 tsp vanilla

Spread over baked muffins and carefully broil 4 inches from top burner until melted and bubbly.

SPREADS... delicious on split muffins

Sweet Orange
1/4 cup butter
1/2 cup icing sugar
1/2 orange (juice & grated rind)

Rich Fruit Butter
1 cup butter
2 Tbsp icing sugar
2 Tbsp grated orange or lemon rind or
1 cup fresh fruit puréed

Beat rind (or purée) into butter. Beat in sugar. Chill.

Mexican Corn

TEMP. 425°F
TIME 25 minutes
MAKES 18 large muffins

Peppy... a change from conventional cornbread... good with chili.

- 1 **cup cornmeal**
- 1 **cup all-purpose flour**
- 1 **Tbsp baking powder**
- 1 **tsp salt**
- ½ **tsp baking soda**
- ½ **tsp white sugar**
- 1 **onion**
- 2 **red chili peppers (dried are fine)**
- ½ **sweet green pepper**
- 2 **eggs**
- 1 **cup buttermilk**
- ½ **cup vegetable oil**
- 1 **cup grated sharp cheese**
- 1 **cup canned cream-style corn**

1. In large bowl mix cornmeal, flour, baking powder, salt, soda & sugar.
2. In electric blender purée the onion, peppers, eggs & buttermilk.
3. Pour into dry mixture together with oil, cheese & corn.
4. Stir until blended.
5. Fill muffin cups and bake.

25

Old Cheddar

TEMP. 425° F
TIME 20 minutes (15 min./small)
MAKES 12 large muffins (24 small)

*Buttermilk is the secret... large size with soup...
small size with salad.*

2 **cups all-purpose flour**
⅓ **cup white sugar (¼ C - less sweet)**
1 **Tbsp baking powder**
½ **tsp baking soda**
1 **cup grated old cheddar cheese (yellow for color)**
¼ **cup vegetable oil**
1 **cup buttermilk**
1 **egg**

1. Sift together dry ingredients.
2. Stir in grated cheese.
3. Beat oil, buttermilk and egg.
4. Pour into dry ingredients.
5. Stir to blend.
6. Fill muffin cups and bake.

 If desired, sprinkle batter with grated cheese
and paprika.

26

Miracle Date Nut

TEMP. 375° F
TIME 20 minutes
MAKES 12 large muffins

Moist and delicious... from Lynda who uses her mother's cast-iron pans for huge puffy muffins.

1½ **cups chopped dates**
　2 **tsp baking soda**
　1 **cup boiling water**
　1 **cup miracle whip salad dressing**
　¾ **cup brown sugar**
　½ **cup natural bran**
1½ **cups all-purpose flour**
　½ **tsp cinnamon**
　½ **tsp nutmeg**

1. In large bowl pour boiling water over dates and soda.
2. Mix and allow to cool.
3. Add salad dressing and brown sugar. Mix well.
4. Add bran.
5. Sift in flour and spices.
6. Stir to blend.
7. Fill muffin cups and bake.

Add crunch with ¼ cup chopped nuts.

Snappy Ginger

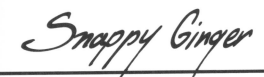

TEMP. 350° F
TIME 25 minutes (18 min./small)
MAKES 12 - 14 large muffins (30 small)

Here's a timesaver... double recipe... fill 2 dozen muffin cups... bake remainder in square cake pan for 45 minutes and presto - fresh gingerbread!

½ **cup vegetable oil**
¼ **cup brown sugar**
¼ **cup white sugar**
1 **egg**
1 **cup molasses**
3 **cups all-purpose flour**
1½ **tsp baking soda**
1 **tsp cinnamon**
1 **tsp ginger**
½ **tsp cloves**
¾ **tsp salt**
1 **cup hot water**

1. In large beater bowl, cream oil & sugars.
2. Add egg and molasses. Beat well.
3. Sift dry ingredients together.
4. Add to creamed mixture alternately with hot water.
5. Fill muffin cups and bake.

Refrigerator Ginger

TEMP. 375° F
TIME 30 minutes
MAKES 3 dozen large muffins

An alternative for ginger lovers...
bake when convenient.

1 **cup shortening**	4 **cups all-purpose flour**
1 **cup white sugar**	4 **tsp ginger**
1 **cup molasses**	1 **tsp allspice**
4 **eggs**	½ **tsp nutmeg**
2 **tsp baking soda**	2 **cups raisins**
1 **cup buttermilk**	**(soaked in water)**

1. Cream shortening; add sugar. Beat until fluffy.
2. Stir in molasses.
3. Add eggs, one at a time. Beat well after each addition.
4. Dissolve soda in buttermilk.
5. Combine flour and spices.
6. Add to creamed mixture alternately with buttermilk, beating well after each addition.
7. Drain raisins. Stir into batter.
8. **Cover and store in fridge for 24 hours before baking. Do not remix.**
9. Batter will keep up to 3 weeks.

29

Lemon

TEMP. 400°F
TIME 15 - 20 minutes
MAKES 10 - 12 large muffins

Perfect for tea or for dessert with berries and cream.

2 **cups all-purpose flour**
½ **cup plus 2 Tbsp white sugar**
1 **Tbsp baking powder**
1 **tsp salt**
½ **cup butter (margarine)**
½ **cup fresh lemon juice**
2 **eggs**
Grated rind of 1 or 2 lemons

1. Combine flour, ½ C sugar, baking powder and salt. Blend well.
2. Melt butter. Remove from heat and stir in lemon juice, rind and eggs.
3. Stir egg mixture into dry ingredients until well moistened.
4. Fill muffin cups. Sprinkle tops with white sugar. Bake until lightly browned.

Maple Walnut

TEMP. 425° F
TIME 20 minutes (until golden brown)
MAKES 12 large muffins

*The 'chelsea bun' of muffins... best served warm...
developed by Susan Lee, freelance food writer for
The London Free Press and The Brantford
Expositor.*

 2 **Tbsp butter**
 ½ **cup maple syrup**
 ¼ **cup coarsely chopped walnuts**
 2 **cups all-purpose flour**
 3 **tsp baking powder**
 1 **tsp cinnamon**
 ½ **tsp salt**
 3 **Tbsp maple syrup**
 1 **cup milk**
 ¼ **cup vegetable oil**
 1 **egg**

1. Warm butter and syrup together in small pan.
2. Place 2 tsp of this mixture in each of twelve large
   muffin pans.
3. Sprinkle 1 tsp nuts into each pan.
4. Into large bowl, sift flour, baking powder, salt
   and cinnamon.
5. Stir together syrup, milk, oil and egg.
6. Pour liquid into dry ingredients and stir just
   until moistened.
7. Fill prepared pans ⅔ full and bake.
8. When baked, up-turn on cooling rack placed over
   foil to allow syrup to flow over muffins. Remove
   from pans while hot before syrup hardens.

31

Mincemeat Bran

TEMP. 375° F
TIME 18 - 20 minutes
MAKES 24 large muffins

Bea keeps these on hand for Peter when farm chores are finished.

2 **eggs, beaten**
¾ **cup vegetable oil**
¾ **cup white sugar**
¼ **cup molasses or brown sugar**
2 **cups milk**
1½ **cups mincemeat**
2¼ **cups all-purpose flour**
1¼ **cups natural bran**
2 **tsp baking powder**
2 **tsp baking soda**
1 **tsp salt**

1. Beat eggs, oil and sugar.
2. Add molasses, milk and mincemeat and beat together.
3. Blend in dry ingredients.
4. Fill muffin cups and bake.

 Leftover batter may be stored covered in the fridge for a few days.

TEMP. 375° F
TIME 30 minutes
MAKES 12 large muffins

Muffins don't have to be sweet... a different taste for brunch or supper.

3 **Tbsp margarine**
½ **lb. mushrooms; finely chopped (3 cups)**
1 **cup whole-wheat flour**
1 **cup all-purpose flour**
3 **tsp baking powder**
2 **tsp white sugar**
½ **tsp salt**
1 **cup grated old cheddar cheese**
¾ **cup milk**
2 **eggs**

1. Heat margarine in fry pan. Cook-stir mushrooms quickly until golden & no moisture left.
2. Sift dry ingredients into bowl.
3. Add cheese and toss until coated.
4. Beat milk and eggs.
5. Add to dry ingredients with mushrooms.
6. Mix until blended.
7. Fill muffin cups and bake.

Marmalade

TEMP. 400°F
TIME 25 minutes
MAKES 12 large muffins

An unexpected surprise ... a rich orange taste.
Watch carefully - these may brown quickly.

2 **cups all-purpose flour**
½ **cup white sugar**
1 **Tbsp baking powder**
½ **tsp salt**
⅔ **cup raisins**
⅓ **cup sunflower seeds (or nuts)**
½ **cup undiluted frozen orange juice (thawed)**
1 **egg**
⅓ **cup margarine (softened or melted)**
¾ **cup marmalade (we use orange)**

1. Sift dry ingredients into large bowl.
2. Stir in raisins and seeds.
3. In small bowl, mix together juice, egg, margarine and marmalade.
4. Add liquid to dry ingredients and stir only until moistened.
5. Fill muffin cups and bake.

 Substitute 1 cup grated cheese for seeds.

Orange Date

TEMP. 400°F
TIME 20 minutes
MAKES 12 large muffins

Try to resist eating a second... our cookbook would not be complete without this favorite from southwestern Ontario.

1 **medium-large orange**
½ **cup orange juice**
½ **cup chopped dates**
1 **egg**
½ **cup margarine (room temp.)**
1½ **cups all-purpose flour**
 (or 1 C + ½ C whole-wheat)
1 **tsp baking soda**
1 **tsp baking powder**
¾ **cup white sugar**
¾ **tsp salt**

1. Cut orange in eighths, remove seeds, put in blender.
2. Add orange juice and dates. Blend until liquified.
3. Add egg and margarine. Blend again.
4. Into large bowl, sift dry ingredients.
5. Add blender mixture to flour mixture.
6. Stir to blend.
7. Fill muffin cups and bake.

35

Orange Pineapple

TEMP. 400°F
TIME 20 minutes
MAKES 12 large muffins

From Mary's farm kitchen in Komoka... orange and pineapple - a friendly combination.

½ **cup all-bran cereal**
½ **cup orange juice**
½ **cup shortening (or margarine)**
½ **cup white sugar**
1 **egg**
1¾ **cups all-purpose flour**
2 **tsp baking powder**
½ **tsp baking soda**
½ **tsp salt**
¼ **cup milk**
1 **cup drained crushed pineapple**

1. In small bowl, mix bran cereal and orange juice.
2. In large bowl beat shortening and sugar.
3. Add egg to creamed mixture. Beat until light.
4. Sift in dry ingredients alternately with milk and bran mixture.
5. Stir in crushed pineapple.
6. Fill muffin cups and bake.

Orange Oatmeal

TEMP. 350° F
TIME 20 minutes
MAKES 14 large muffins

What could be better for breakfast than orange juice and oatmeal... but good for snacks anytime.

 1 **cup rolled oats**
½ **cup orange juice (add grated rind if fresh orange used)**
½ **cup boiling water**
⅓ **cup margarine**
½ **cup brown sugar**
½ **cup white sugar**
 2 **eggs, beaten**
 1 **cup raisins**
 1 **cup all-purpose flour**
 1 **tsp baking powder**
 1 **tsp baking soda**
 1 **tsp salt**
 1 **tsp vanilla**

1. In small bowl, soak rolled oats in orange juice (and rind) and boiling water for 15 minutes.
2. In large bowl, cream together margarine and sugars.
3. Beat in eggs and oats mixture.
4. Stir in raisins and remaining ingredients.
5. Fill muffin cups and bake.

Pumpkin Orange

TEMP.   400°F
TIME   18 - 20 minutes
MAKES   12 large muffins

Orange adds zip to the pumpkin.

1¾ **cups all-purpose flour**
2½ **tsp baking powder**
½ **tsp baking soda**
½ **tsp salt**
1 **tsp cinnamon**
¼ **tsp nutmeg**
¼ **tsp ginger**
¼ **tsp mace**
⅔ **cup brown sugar**
¼ **cup chopped raisins**
¼ **cup chopped walnuts**

¼ **cup vegetable oil**
½ **cup milk**
½ **cup orange juice**
1 **egg**
1 **tsp orange peel**
(or more)
¾ **cup canned pumpkin**
(without added spices)
TOPPING MIXTURE
1 **tsp pumpkin-pie spice**
2 **Tbsp white sugar**

1. Sift dry ingredients into large bowl.
2. Stir in brown sugar, raisins and walnuts.
3. Beat together oil, milk, juice, egg, peel
   and pumpkin.
4. Pour into dry mixture. Stir to blend.
5. Fill muffin cups.
6. Sprinkle topping mixture on batter and bake.

Try ½ C sunflower seeds instead of raisins
and walnuts.

Pineapple Gems

TEMP. 350°F
TIME 20 - 25 minutes
MAKES 12 - 14 large muffins

For the person who is tired of bran.

½ **cup butter or margarine (room temp.)**
⅔ **cup white sugar**
1 **egg**
2 **cups all-purpose flour**
1 **tsp baking powder**
½ **tsp baking soda**
½ **tsp salt**
½ **tsp cinnamon**
¼ **tsp cloves**
1 **cup crushed pineapple with juice**

1. Cream butter, sugar and egg until light.
2. Sift dry ingredients together.
3. Add to creamed mixture alternately with pineapple.
   (Begin and end with dry ingredients)
4. Fill muffin cups and bake.

 Add ½ cup coconut — good!

Peanut Butter

TEMP. 375° F
TIME 25 minutes
MAKES 12 large muffins

These disappear very quickly on baking day.

⅓ **cup margarine (part shortening)**
¼ **cup brown sugar**
¼ **cup white sugar**
½ **cup crunchy peanut butter**
1 **egg**
2 **cups all-purpose flour**
2 **tsp baking powder**
1 **tsp baking soda**
1 **cup milk**
⅓ **cup chopped chocolate chips**

1. With electric mixer cream margarine, sugars, peanut butter & egg.
2. Sift flour, baking powder & soda and add alternately with milk until blended.
3. Stir in chocolate chips.
4. Fill muffin cups and bake.

40

TEMP. 400°F
TIME 20 minutes
MAKES 16 large muffins

Years ago westerners referred to prunes as 'CPR Strawberries' because of the elegant way railroad dining cars served stewed prunes and cream!

2 **cups all-purpose flour**
2 **tsp baking powder**
1 **tsp salt**
1 **tsp cinnamon**
1 **tsp baking soda**
1 **cup brown sugar**
¼ **cup wheat germ**
1½ **cups chopped prunes**
⅓ **cup vegetable oil**
1¼ **cups buttermilk**
1 **egg**
1 **tsp vanilla**
   TOPPING
2 **Tbsp poppy seeds (optional)**

1. Sift flour, baking powder, salt, cinnamon, soda into large bowl.
2. Add brown sugar and wheat germ. Stir.
3. Stir in prunes.
4. Beat oil, buttermilk, egg, vanilla.
5. Add to dry mixture. Stir to blend.
6. Fill muffin cups.
7. If desired, sprinkle poppy seeds on batter and bake.

41

Boiled Raisin

TEMP. 375° F
TIME 20 - 25 minutes
MAKES 12 large muffins

An old-fashioned recipe...
popular with our grandmothers.

1½ **cups raisins**
1½ **cups water**
 ⅔ **cup brown sugar**
 ½ **cup shortening**
 1 **egg**
1½ **cups all-purpose flour**
 1 **tsp baking powder**
 1 **tsp baking soda**
 1 **tsp vanilla**

1. Boil raisins in water for 20 minutes.
2. Cream sugar, shortening and egg.
3. Add cooled, drained raisins, plus ½ C raisin water to sugar mixture.
4. Add sifted dry ingredients to first mixture.
5. Add vanilla and stir until blended.
6. Fill muffin cups and bake.

42

Sugar and Spice

TEMP. 350° F
TIME 15 minutes
MAKES 24 medium-small muffins

We fill pans ⅓ full for these doughnut-like tidbits... small tart pans are another idea.

1¾ **cups all-purpose flour**
1½ **tsp baking powder**
½ **tsp salt**
½ **tsp nutmeg**
⅓ **cup vegetable oil**
¾ **cup white sugar (first amount)**
1 **egg**
¾ **cup milk**
AFTER BAKING
⅔ **cup melted butter or margarine**
¾ **cup white sugar (second amount)**
1 **tsp cinnamon**

1. Sift together flour, baking powder, salt, nutmeg.
2. Beat oil, ¾ cup sugar, egg, milk.
3. Add this mixture to dry ingredients.
4. Stir to blend.
5. Fill **greased** muffin cups about ⅓ full of batter. (Do not use paper baking cups.)
6. When baked, remove immediately from pans.
7. Melt butter in saucepan.
8. While hot, dip each muffin in melted butter then roll in mixture of ¾ cup sugar and cinnamon.

43

Penny's Seed

TEMP. 400° F
TIME 20 minutes
MAKES 12 large muffins

Delightfully speckled with seeds and nuts.

1½ **cups all-purpose flour**
½ **cup whole-wheat flour**
1 **tsp baking powder**
1 **tsp baking soda**
½ **tsp salt**
¾ **cup brown sugar**
½ **cup chopped nuts**
2 **Tbsp wheat germ**
2 **Tbsp sesame seeds**
2 **Tbsp poppy seeds**
1 **egg**
1 **cup buttermilk**
¼ **cup vegetable oil**

1. Sift flour, baking powder, soda and salt into large bowl.
2. Stir in sugar, nuts, wheat germ and seeds.
3. Beat together egg, buttermilk and oil.
4. Pour into dry ingredients.
5. Stir to blend.
6. Fill muffin cups and bake.

44

Thames Trail

TEMP. 350°F
TIME 20 minutes
MAKES 18 large muffins

*Nourishment while you're hiking... take your
"Trail Mix" in a muffin.*

1½ **cups very hot water**	½ **tsp baking soda**
¼ **cup molasses**	1½ **tsp salt**
½ **cup natural bran**	⅓ **cup vegetable oil**
½ **cup rolled oats**	2 **large eggs**
3 **Tbsp white sugar**	2 **tsp vanilla**
3 **Tbsp brown sugar**	½ **cup coconut**
½ **cup all-purpose flour**	½ **cup walnuts**
½ **cup whole wheat flour**	½ **cup sunflower seeds**
¼ **cup graham flour**	1 **cup raisins**
½ **cup skim milk powder**	½ **cup chopped dates**
3 **Tbsp wheat germ**	½ **cup chopped apricots**
1 **tsp baking powder**	**(optional)**

1. In large beater bowl combine water and molasses.
2. Add bran and oats. Soak for 15 minutes.
3. In another bowl combine sugars, flours, milk
   powder, wheat germ, baking powder, soda
   and salt.
4. To the soaked bran-oats, add and beat oil,
   eggs, vanilla.
5. Add dry ingredients. Combine thoroughly.
6. Stir in nuts and fruit.
7. Fill muffin cups and bake.

45

Zucchini Whole-Wheat

TEMP. 400°F
TIME 20 minutes
MAKES 9 large muffins

A 'biscuit' to serve warm with homemade soup for a nourishing lunch.

2 **cups whole-wheat flour**
¾ **tsp salt**
2 **tsp baking powder**
2 **Tbsp white sugar**
¼ **tsp mace**
1 **egg**
½ **cup milk**
2 **Tbsp melted margarine**
1 **cup grated zucchini**
TOPPING MIXTURE
½ **tsp cinnamon**
1 **Tbsp white sugar**

1. Mix dry ingredients together.
2. Beat together egg, milk, margarine.
3. Pour into flour mixture. Stir to blend.
4. Stir in zucchini.
5. Fill muffin cups and bake.

Zucchini Cheese Bran

TEMP. 425°F
TIME 20 minutes
MAKES 12 large muffins

A meal in a muffin!... for lunch - split in half and fill with ham, lettuce and sharp mayonnaise.

1 **cup all-bran cereal**	1 **cup whole-wheat flour**
¾ **cup buttermilk**	2½ **tsp baking powder**
⅓ **cup brown sugar**	½ **tsp baking soda**
⅓ **cup margarine**	½ **tsp salt**
(melted or softened)	1 **cup grated cheese**
1 **egg**	**(old or medium)**
	1 **cup grated zucchini**

1. In large bowl soak cereal in buttermilk.
2. Stir in sugar, margarine and egg.
3. Sift in flour, baking powder, soda and salt.
4. Add grated cheese and zucchini.
5. Stir until moistened.
6. Fill muffin cups.
7. Sprinkle a little grated cheese on batter and bake.

Try 1 cup chopped raw broccoli or ½ cup drained, chopped pickle in place of zucchini and increase buttermilk to 1 cup.

47

The Last Word in Muffins.

TEMP. 350° F
TIME 1 hour
MAKES 2 one-pound coffee cans

Two Mighty Muffins baked in coffee cans!

1½ **cups white sugar**
½ **cup vegetable oil**
2 **eggs**
⅓ **cup water**
1¾ **cups all-purpose flour**
1½ **tsp cinnamon**
1 **tsp nutmeg**
1 **tsp baking soda**
½ **tsp salt**
1 **cup canned pumpkin**
 (without added seasonings)
½ **cup chopped pecans**
½ **cup raisins**

1. In electric mixer bowl beat sugar, oil, eggs and water until combined.
2. Sift into this mixture the flour and spices.
3. Mix until moistened.
4. Stir in pumpkin, pecans and raisins.
5. Spoon batter into 2 greased and floured one-pound coffee cans.
6. Bake until wooden pick inserted in center comes out clean.
7. Let cool in cans for 10 minutes before removing "muffins".

48

For metric recipes you will need metric measures. For recipes such as the ones in this book you can continue to use your old familiar measures or you can use the conversions listed below.

Metric measuring spoons are called "small measures".

— For 1 Tablespoon use the 15mL small measure
— For 1 teaspoon use the 5mL small measure
— For ½ teaspoon use the 2mL small measure
— For ¼ teaspoon use the 1mL small measure

Metric measuring cups are called "dry measures"

— For 1 cup use the 250mL dry measure
— For ½ cup use the 125mL dry measure
— For ¼ cup use the 50mL dry measure
— For ⅓ cup use 3 fillings of the 25mL small measure

Metric liquid cups are called "liquid measures".

— For 1 cup use the 250mL liquid measure
— For 2 cups use the 500mL liquid measure
— For 4 cups use the 1000mL liquid measure
  (1000mL = 1 litre)

Although these conversions are not absolutely accurate they are the accepted replacements and should cause no problem with our recipes.

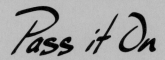

"HAPPY" LITTLE GIFTS – FOR YOURSELF OR FRIENDS. . .
Take advantage of the 5-book offer

SALADS   (Mix or Match)   MUFFINS

Make cheques or money order to: Muffins Publishing Inc.
2 Westview Drive
London, Ontario N6A 2Y3

If you would like to order a book, simply fill out the form with the complete information. (Prices indicate the cost of the book plus shipping.)

If you're giving this book to friends, we can mail directly to them from our office.

Clearly print gift addresses as well as sender's name and address, and send with cheque or money order.

- [ ] 1 book $5.95 + $1 = $6.95
- [ ] 2 books $11.90 + $2 = $13.90
- [ ] 3 books $17.95 + $3 = $20.85
- [ ] 4 books $23.80 + $4 = $27.80
- [ ] A package of 5 books sent to one address, $5.50 x 5 = $27.50 + $3.50 = $31.00
- [ ] 5 Book Offer – (Different addresses) $5.50 x 5 = $27.50 + $5 = $32.50

U.S. Orders Payable in U.S. Funds

COMPLETE ALL ADDRESS INFORMATION BELOW FOR CANPAR OR CANADA POST

- [ ] **SENDER**   - [ ] **SEND BOOK(S) DIRECTLY TO ME**

Name (Please Print) _____

Mail Address _____

Street Address _____

City _____ Prov. _____ Code _____

_____ copies of SALADS... a cookbook   Phone _____

_____ copies of MUFFINS... a cookbook.

Please send cookbook(s) directly to the address below.

Name (Please Print) _____

Mail Address _____

Street Address _____

City _____ Prov. _____ Code _____

_____ copies of SALADS... a cookbook   Phone _____

_____ copies of MUFFINS... a cookbook.